D. M. (Dulcina Mason) Jordan, Dulcina Mason Jordan

Rosemary Leaves

D. M. (Dulcina Mason) Jordan, Dulcina Mason Jordan

Rosemary Leaves

ISBN/EAN: 9783744685238

Printed in Europe, USA, Canada, Australia, Japan

Cover: Foto ©Thomas Meinert / pixelio.de

More available books at **www.hansebooks.com**

ROSEMARY LEAVES

BY

MRS. D. M. JORDAN

" *There 's Rosemary: that 's for remembrance,*"—SHAKESPEARE

CINCINNATI
ROBERT CLARKE & COMPANY
1873

AFFECTIONATELY DEDICATED

TO

MY MOTHER

AND

SISTERS.

CONTENTS.

PREFACE.

I 'HAVE culled from the garden of fancy
  The greenest of all her leaves,
And bound them together in gladness
  As the harvester garners his sheaves;
And out of the waning autumn,
  When dead leaves rustle down,
I bring *my* leaves of remembrance,
  The brow that I love, to crown.

ROSEMARY, sweet and bitter,
  Gathered with tenderest care;
Twined with an earnest purpose
  And bound with a thread of prayer:
Fragrant with sweetest meaning
  To hearts that love me well;
Only leaves that will perish
  Where Friendship owns no spell.

You who have pressed sweet roses
  In the leaves of some volume dear—
Keeping the fragrance of summer
  Thro' all the days of the year—

Take from my garland of fancy
One leaf to wear in your heart,
To hold me in fond remembrance,
From the other leaves apart.

TO POESY.

WITH reverent steps I come, and low-bowed head,
To the charmed presence of my bright ideal,
Who sits enthroned in the sweet realm of song—
A queen of fancy, beautiful and real
As ever yet inspired the tuneful lays
Of wandering minstrel in the courtly days.

Not to the Poet knights—who sweetly sing
In palaces to kingly court and throng,
Bearing brave honors on their manly breasts
And wearing laurel crowns—do I belong ;
But rather would I sing a simple strain,
To win some mourner from his dream of pain.

Not on the height of the fair mount of song,
Where full-voiced singers chant in rhythmic strains
The songs that echo in the world's great throng,
Winning the meed of praise and golden gains,
But in the valley, where the daisies grow,
I sing such songs as untaught ears may know.

Songs of the summer days, when full and clear,
   The robin's note sets all the world in tune ;
When yellow fields bow to the reaper's tread,
   And bees go singing 'mid the flowers of June,
And wings, as free as thought, are cleaving thro'
The upper ocean's depths of softest blue ;

And dreamy days, when summer leaves are dead,
   And failing streams sing thro' the meadows brown ;
When dim woods hold a whisper of the past,
   And ripened fruits are softly dropping down,
And the tired earth, released from summer's care,
Sits sunning in the glowing autumn air :

Of flowers that grow unnamed in shady spots,
   And reeds that dally with the rippling stream ;
Where cool green mosses hide the wasting tree
   From the full glory of the noontide beam,
And silence, like a presence, thrills the air
Like the sweet rapture of unuttered prayer.

No voice have I for thrilling clarion strains,
   And trumpet's tones to call the world to arms,
To battle for great deeds of sounding fame
   Beyond the peaceful valley's quiet charms ;
But where the dim aisles of the forest lead
To nature's shrines, I tune my humble reed.

Sweet poesy! thy realm of heavenly song
  I enter with a sense akin to dread,
Lest I should fail to utter what I feel,
  And wound the darling of my heart, instead
Of crowning her with simple wild-wood flowers,
Breathing the sweetness of the summer hours.

And yet, the heart's great mysteries divine
  Are oft'nest whispered low by faltering tongue ;
The great earth yieldeth up her harvest wealth
  As silently as summer winds are flung
From clouds that sweep above the sleeping earth,
Dropping the seeds for some new summer's birth.

So, if I lead some weary dust-stained feet
  To pleasant fields, and forests cool and green,
Where God's sweet peace rests like a benison
  The noisy marts of busy worlds between,
My low-voiced song shall not have been in vain :
I shall have won some heart away from pain.

And if some heart, made happier by my song,
  Take up its burden with a better grace,
Where worthier songs have failed to lift it up
  From the deep mists to nature's glorious face—
If I may lead it to a heavenward view,
Sweet poesy! to me, thou art divinely true.

A WINTER VISION.

TO-DAY, in thoughtful mood, I walked
 Within the forest dull and brown,
Whose leafless trees like sentries stand
 Beyond the borders of the town.
No sound of life was in the air—
 The grave is not more cold and still—
No rustle of sweet summer leaves,
 Nor any song of bird or rill.

Only dumb silence over all
 Kept watch and ward, with soundless tread,
Waiting for folded buds to break
 In resurrection from the dead.
Whence came the presence, all unseen ;
 The flood of memories, sad and sweet ;
Or fancied scent of violets blue,
 When none were blooming near my feet?

How shall I know what hidden cord
 By some mysterious hand was swept,
To stir my inmost being through
 With memories which so long had slept—

With memories which I thought were dead,
  And buried beyond reach of pain ;
And grief, whose bitterness once drained,
  I never thought to taste again.

Grief never dies, but grows a part
  Of the strong soul from day to day.
At first by outward signs 't is moved,
  But slow and sure it learns the way,
And surely learns how weak and slight
  Are outward holds, and how alone,
Aye, even from the help of heaven,
  Its bitterness is all its own.

IN MARCH.

I HAVE been looking forth thro' tears to day,
Into brown sodden fields, and forests bare,
And murmuring that the fickle spring is late,
And that the meadows are not green and fair.

I have been looking back through open doors
That led me out to memory's haunted dell,
Where, from the silence of these lonesome days,
I find a happiness too sweet to tell.

In the brown earth I see some spikes of green,
And yet the hollows are all filled with snow.
The crocus looks upon a frozen world ;
I know not how the dainty thing can grow.

Chill, homeless birds await the sunny days
In frozen fields and in the leafless trees ;
And shall I murmur that my spring-time waits,
When He will care for even such as these?

Yet I am restless for the May blue sky,
The apple blossoms and the song of birds,
The sweet, wild beauty of the rustling woods,
The tinkling bell among the happy herds.

Eager for running brooks, so free and wild—
   Longing to climb the breezy, sunny hill,
And follow on to where the sunset skies
   Shut in the night so beautiful and still.

Tired, oh so tired of cold, gray, sunless days,
   Across whose nights I see the summer's glow—
Beloved pictures, warm with happy life,
   Beyond the ghostly regions of the snow.

APRIL.

THE tearful sky wept all day long
      In token of the April weather,
And something in my heart o'erflowed—
   The clouds and I were sad together.
But when the day was near its close,
   The sun set all the earth a-shining,
And in my heart the heavy cloud
   Unfolded all its silver lining.

The rain had brightened all the slopes,
   Where tender leaves of green were springing,
And from each jewel-spangled bough
   The happy troops of birds were singing ;
And arching o'er the shining earth,
   The radiant bow unveiled its glory,
Repeating to the world below,
   The promise, and the wondrous story.

The day that wept in rain and tears,
   Went smiling thro' the gate of even,
And on the bridge that spanned the sky
   My heart went to the door of heaven—

Went up in songs of happy praise,
  For all the beauty and the sweetness
That crowned the changeful April day,
  And filled my soul with such completeness.

THE SONG THAT THE ROBIN SINGS.

UNDER my window a robin is singing,
   Swayed by the tremulous breath of the wind,
Rocked to and fro 'mid the emerald branches,
   Free, with a freedom my soul can not find.
What can it be in the robin's low trilling
   That touches my heart with a vague unrest,
Waking the echoes in memory's chamber
   Of a beautiful dream that was ne'er confessed?

Many a May-time has blossomed and faded—
   Oft have the robins come and flown—
Since in my bosom the melody wakened
   That thrilled just now at the wild bird's tone.
Many a brilliant and airy castle
   Has faded out, like the stars at dawn,
And the master hand of my heart's sweet music
   A wanderer over the earth has gone.

And yet when the May comes round in beauty,
   And the hedges are touched with tender green—
When the robin tells the same sweet story
   She told when my years were but sixteen,

I am filled with a sad and restless feeling,
　A wandering into the silent past—
A wondering why the glad May-season
　Of life and love should so soon be past.

And though I am only an idle dreamer,
　I know that life hath a noble goal ;
As a vesture, folded away in darkness,
　We may not bury the human soul—
Wonderful soul, with a life eternal,
　Full of bright and beautiful things,
Why art thou thrilled to the inmost center
　By the simple song that the robin sings?

"DOLCE FAR NIENTE."

MY thoughts are on the wing to-day,
   Nor would I stay them if I might;
For many an olive branch of hope,
   They 've gathered in their restless flight.
The harvest-fields are thick with grain,
   Swift ripening 'neath the skies of June,
And o'er the scented clover-field
   The. wild bee hums a happy tune.

Along the crumbling garden-wall
   The crimson roses nod in glee,
And robin'song and bluebird note
   Mingle in sweetest harmony.
Across the fields of waving grain,
   The billowy ripples ebb and flow
Like waves upon a summer sea
   Swept lightly by the winds that blow.

My feet have wandered far to-day
   Away from busy haunts of life,
With soul attuned to nature's voice,
   Forgetting all the din and strife ;

And in this charmed and sweet repose
  O'ercanopied by forest trees.
Whose loving arms are interlaced
  In playful dalliance with the breeze,

I 've watched the slowly gliding stream,
  And listened to the ripple's flow.
The while I heard, unconsciously,
  Sweet echoes from the long ago,
So softly set to happy chords,
  That sing themselves in tender tune
A melody of thankfulness
  For all the sweetness of the June.

The shadows lengthen while I gaze,
  The gold is fading from the sky,
And sailing low on weary wing
  The wandering swallows homeward fly.
The tinkle of a far-off bell
  Comes faintly on the evening air,
And o'er the unfledged nest I hear
  The mother bird at vesper prayer.

A purple mist creeps up the sky
  Where late the clouds were flaming gold.
And fainter sounds the robin's trill
  Above the brood her wings enfold.

With lingering feet I quit the spot,
Still looking back with many a sigh.
Sweet dream, with happy memories fraught,
Sweet summer-day of June, good-bye!

NOONDAY IN AUGUST.

A SLOPING hill, a shaded bank,
   A sun midway upon the sky ;
A lazy stream, where cattle drink,
   Or in the cooling shadows lie ;
A dusty highway gleaming white,
   Bordered by untrimmed hedges green ;
A hum of happy insect life,
   And fluttering wings of golden sheen ;

And on the sky the white clouds lie
   Like ships becalmed in tropic seas.
With motionless and idle sail,
   Unstirred by any passing breeze.
A hush is on the busy town,
   And passing feet make echoes loud
Upon the foot-worn pavement, where
   At morning went the hurrying crowd.

The leaves hang limp upon the vine,
   The flowers have closed their fragrant cells,
The murmuring bee on droning wing
   No longer seeks the honeyed wells :

The river scarcely seems to glide—
·   So placid is the glassy stream,
Reflecting in its crystal deeps
    The glory of the noonday beam.

Beneath the elm tree's cooling shade,
    The reaper seeks his noontide rest,
Lulled sweetly by the twittering song
    Of birds above the unfledged nest;
And here beneath this spreading beech,
    My book lies open and unread—
My soul is in the lotus land,
    My senses on its blossoms fed.

I see the world through drowsy eyes,
    And hear its noises faint and far;
My happy heart has flown away,
    And sails through space like some glad star.
I link the present with the past
    So closely, that I almost seem
To live again the vanished hours,
    As one may live them in a dream.

Sweet spirits from the shadowy land
    Have set their seal upon my eyes,
And on my inner ear there falls
    A music from the upper skies.

No sound to mar the sweet repose,
No sight to break my happy rest,
In perfect peacefulness I lie—
A child, upon a mother's breast.

SEPTEMBER.

O MOON of golden fruit and garnered grain—
  Of skies and peaks that melt in mist together,
And streams that sing in murmurs soft and low—
  A tender requiem for the summer weather !
Where late the winds went plowing through the field,
  Breaking the grain apart in shining furrows.
The brown quail pipes his cheery note of song,
  And the sleek mole beneath the stubble burrows.

The hush of slumber rests upon the earth ;
  The clouds are still, as if in silent blessing :
And the soft winds that sweep the fading field
  Have in their whispers something of caressing.
Along the borders of the dusty road
  The silvery thistledown is lightly drifting :
And changeful colors sweep the landscape o'er,
  Like magic pictures on the canvass shifting.

The bee sings low amid the scented grass,
  And golden sunflowers watch the sun's slow turning ;
The grapes are purpling on the clustering vine
  Quick with the prisoned wine within them burning ;

The lark calls sweetly from the far-off hills,
  And the slow hawk sails by with dreamy motion ;
The sun rides thro' the depth of softest blue,—
  A blazing ship upon a tropic ocean.

Sweet golden days that wait the summer's death,
  Like tender watchers o'er a loved one's slumber,
Ye stand between the lost one and the grave,
  With consolations that our griefs outnumber,—
The song of swallows twittering from the eaves,
  Of new-fledged birds that plume their wings for flying,
And forests robed in gold and purple state,
  Like some grand king who waits the hour for dying.

We welcomed May with all her changing skies,
  And hailed with joy the queenly month of flowers ;
Counting some blessing in each fleeting day,
  Telling them on a rosary of hours.
Some idle tears must fall above the past,
  For all the sweet dead days that we remember ;
But with the garnered treasures in our grasp,
  We drink the golden wine of bright September.

OCTOBER.

THE light that dyes
October's skies
Gleams opaline and many hued,
Like rays that drop from Paradise
By earthly mists and clouds subdued.

The sunset glow
In crimson flow
Turns lake and river into blood,
While far and near, all things appear
Transfigured with a golden flood.

On level wing
The swallows swing
Above the meadows dull and brown.
While all the air in silent prayer
Drops from the sky a blessing down.

The orchards flush
In deepest blush,
And scatter largess rich and free.
While from each limb goes up a hymn
Of praise for the full-fruited tree.

The forest bright
Gleams with a light
Of gold and royal tyrian hue,
While through the sky the clouds sail by
Like white ships on a sea of blue.

I know not why
Beneath this sky
Come shadows of a vain regret,
Nor why a tear should tremble here
For what 't were better to forget.

NOVEMBER.

WHAT are the wild winds saying,
    As they sweep thro' the stormy sky,
Or moan 'mid the leafless branches,
    With a sound like a human sigh?
They are telling in mournful whispers
    Of the beautiful summer dead,
Of May and her faded garlands,
    Of June and her roses fled ;

Of the shining days of August,
    And the sweet September glow,
Of the regally crowned October
    With footsteps silent and slow.
They are telling of harvests garnered,
    Of ripened and gathered sheaves,
Of empty nests in the forests
    And under the homestead eaves ;

They are telling of stranded vessels,
    And wrecks upon stormy waves,
Of signal guns on a midnight sea,
    Of cruel and watery graves :

And of leaves that drift in the valleys.
    And mounds where no grass has grown,
Of beautiful idyls vanished,
    And beautiful visions flown.
Of a year with its joys and sorrows
    That Time, like a sheaf hath bound,
Leaving no fruit for the gleaner
    On all the desolate ground.

Oh, wind of the wild November,
    A sorrowful voice is thine—
A requiem over the dying year,
    Of the snowy shroud a sign ;
And harvest days that are over,
    When we gathered no golden grain,
And links that are broken forever
    And lost from love's magical chain.

THE YEAR.

A S some tired laborer at the close of day
Watches the light grow gorgeous as it wanes,
And sees as in a dream the sunset gold
  Gild the far steeples and the western panes.
So sits the year, wrapped in the purple haze
  And mellow radiance of autumnal dyes,
Resting amid the trophies of the field
  That ripened under all her summer skies :

Breathing the air from golden-fruited trees,
  Elate with odors from the clust'ring vine
Whose purple fruit drank in the summer's glow,
  To quicken into life the imprisoned wine.
Rich are the hues the fading year puts on.
  Her tyrian mantle and embroidered vest,
Her trailing robe fringed with the autumn flowers,
  And turban with its gorgeous colors dressed.

Across the dull brown field with stately tread
  She walks among the dry and withered leaves,
Where late the scarlet pink flamed thro' the grass,
  Or where the reapers bound the golden sheaves.

Pausing and looking back with many a smile
  Of summer radiance, all too bright to last,
She goes her way across the wintry hills,
  And sends her farewell on December's blast.

Ah ! well for us who hear the sad good-bye
  Each year with something less of tender sorrow,
Who count one weary march toward the day
  Whose perfect light shall have no night nor morrow ;
Who see with undimned sight and cloudless faith,
  The shining Zoar that waits our pilgrim feet,
Beyond the vanishing and changing years,
  Where time with vast eternity shall meet.

"THE SONG OF SEVEN."

POET, sing me a simple rhyme,
   A tale that is true and not a dream :
You may sing of the earthly life of man—
   Could poet ask for a nobler theme?
And I said, Shall I sing the " Song of Seven,"
And its wonderful steps from earth to heaven—
Shall I tell how the mortal finds its way
Out of the darkness into the day,
Out of the shadows into the light,
Out of the finite to infinite?
Have you ever thought of the swaddling bands -
The tender and helpless baby hands?
Have you ever seen the round blank eyes,
Sans speculation and sans surprise,
Of the baby who squares his fists at time
For coming upon him before his prime?
Have you ever seen the little feet,
With the toes like rosebuds, pink and sweet?
Have you thought of the journey that lies before,
Which those little feet must travel o'er?

Have you measured the mountains that must be passed,
From the first footstep to the weary last,
Of the stages that lead through earth to heaven:
This is the first one of the seven.

The second step in his upward climb,
The second round in the ladder of time,
He takes, when armed with satchel and rule,
And resolute steps, he starts to school ;
When he grasps the puzzle of "A, B, C,"
And fights with the giant '· rule of three ;"
When he flounders on through "shillings and pence."
Feeling his way through the dim immense :
Learning each day some wonderful truth.
He passes from boyhood into youth.

Youth, with its glorious hopes and dreams,
Its airy castle of golden gleams,
Its bright ambitions, undimmed, unfaded,
Its love and trust, by doubt unshaded,
Its sighing and singing of tender strains,
Under the loved one's window panes.
Alas ! that the bridge is so short a span,
That divides the life of youth from man !

Man, in all his glory and strength,
He has reached the middle stage at length ;

Strong of purpose and Godlike will,
He sends the lightning o'er vale and hill;
He chains the mighty giant of steam
Whose voice we hear in the whistle's scream ;
He makes broad rivers of tiny rills,
And tunnels the everlasting hills ;
He marshals his armies on field and plain,
And sends his ships o'er the boundless main ;
He plants his flag on mountain and hill,
And sails through the azure sky at will ;
He binds two worlds by the lightning's power,
In the wonderful circle of an hour.

But the sun has passed the meridian line,
The shadows lengthen at day's decline ;
The ears grow weary of noise and strife,
The back grows tired of the burden of life :
And looking back where the journey begun,
Over many a battle lost and won,
He is ready to say, " Behold ! what a span
Are the weary, vanishing days of man."

There cometh a twilight cold and gray,
After the sunlight fades away—
The holy hour of the vesper song,
An hour when the fainting soul grows strong ;
A time when faith leads into light,

When creed and doctrine have vanished quite ;
When he heareth the voice of the Master mild,
" Except ye become as a little child."

Again with the trust of a little child,
He walks in a pathway undefiled,
With feeble step and trembling limb,
While the sounds of life grow strangely dim.
The midnight watch is drawing near,
    The angel waits in the outer hall,
The seven stages of life are passed,
    And he "goeth in at the Bridegroom's call."

LIVING MARTYRS.

THINK you the days of martyrdom are past
  Because the flaming stake and torturing wheel
Send up no stifling smoke or bitter groan,
  The agonies of suffering to reveal?
Or think you that the fagot's flaming pyre,
  Or rack whereon the victim writhed in pain,
Were worse to bear than years of living death
  Without the recompense that martyrs gain?

Better the swift destruction of the fire,
  Turning its victim into ashes gray,—
Ashes, that feel no more the scorching flame,—
  Dust, by the first light zephyr blown away,—
Dust, that can feel not any crushing tread
  Or thrill of anguish under bitter scorn,
Longing to lie among the dreamless dead,
  Or wishing madly it had ne'er been born.

No tears for those who win the martyr's crown
  Through some brief hours of bitter tribulation,
Bearing a heavy cross but for a day,
  To win eternity's great compensation.

Weep for the martyrs walking in your midst,
  Who bear the fire without an outward token,
Who tread the changeless round of daily care,
  Wearing a smile altho' the heart be broken.

I read the signs where fate has traced a meaning
  About the eyes in many a deepened line,
Around the lips where once the smiles were beaming,
  Joyless and void of any hopeful sign.
Weep saddest tears for those who make no moaning;
  The river deepens as it nears the sea;
The noisy brawling brook runs loud and shallow,
  But deepest grief is for eternity.

"DAY UNTO DAY."

IF when the crocus buds unfold their leaves,
And hyacinths make fragrant all the air,
The heart might bud and blossom with new life.
Shedding its yearly husks of worldly care,
Would not the flavor of the fruit be lost,
That needs the suns and storms of patient waiting—
The wisdom that is only won by toil,
And steady purpose ever unabating?

The aloe bears within its secret heart
Through years, in which men crumble into earth,
The snow-white crown of patience, born at last
After a century waiting for its birth.
Great heights are only reached through patient climbing ;
High purposes achieved not, save through pain ;
And years of sacrifice we count as naught,
If some great recompense at last we gain.

See how the earth sends up her bounteous harvests,
Disheartened not by all the winter snows ;
And how the skies put on their May-blue lining,
And summer winds unfold the royal rose.

And if some winter clouds of deep dejection
   Shall chill the bud of promise in the soul,
Blighting it past the hope of resurrection,
   Making it faint this side the wished-for goal—
We know the seed was feeble and imperfect,   ,
   Not one to bear the ripened fruit of years ;
And come again, rejoicing with the harvest,
   Albeit the seeds were sown in bitter tears

Whether your feet are on the toilsome journey
   Up the steep height whose temple is called fame,
Or whether with the spirit's earnest striving,
   The battlements of Heaven you would gain,
It matters not : the same unswerving patience
   That leads you up the rugged heights of time,
Will level for your feet the heavenward journey,
   And fit your brow to wear the crown sublime.
Bloom on, sweet hyacinth and tender crocus,
   First harbingers of golden summer days ;
With patience we await our full fruition,
   With patience, toiling on thro' roughest ways.

LIFE.

WE build our puny works on beds of sand,
    Gilding the roughness with a film of gold ;
The winds loosed from the hollow of his hand
    Sweep o'er the temple, and the tale is told.
We climb the rugged steeps of earthly fame,
    Leaving sweet blossoms in the vale below,
And learn too late that on the upper height
    Is the cold glitter of eternal snow.

We watch and wait, we strive and hope in vain,
    For full fruition of our happy dream ;
The mirage springs afresh still farther on.
    The golden apples are not what they seem.
We bear our crosses with too loud complaint
    As if He could not hear who bore them first ;
And of the paths wherein our feet may tread,
    With stubborn blindness, oft we choose the worst.

Yet, from His human heart He dropped the seed
    That springs eternal in the deathless soul ;
And the dim reachings of our feeble hands
    Are blossoms of the fruit that waits the goal.

And in the tender, erring heart He made,
  With all its faults and burdens of regret,
The imprint of a perfect life is traced,
  The Kingly seal upon its tablet set.

OUT OF THE DEPTHS.

STRANGE, that under a sky of blue,
　　Where clouds of silver and amber float,
And the crescent moon at eve's sweet hour
　　Drifts in the blue like a fairy boat,—
Strange! that under the beautiful sky,
　　Like arms outstretched in holy prayer,
Hearts should ache with a weary load,
　　And break, with the burden of grief and care!

Oh! eyes grown dim with weeping,
　　And cheeks grown pale with tears,
Watching, and hoping, and waiting,
　　Through all the weary years—
Oh! heart grown heavy with aching,
　　And hiding your grief away,
And hands so tired of making
　　Idols of perishing clay—

Shut close, oh weary eyelids!
　　Ye are waiting and watching in vain;
And drop, oh tired fingers,
　　The thread of life's tangled skein!

Be silent, oh heart, whose pulses
Have throbbed with a grief untold !
Take back, oh Giver of Life, from me
The gift that I would not hold !

THE DAYS THAT ARE DEAD.

THE sunlight is bright on the forest and meadow,
   The lark and the robin are trilling their song ;
The daisies and buttercups border the pathway,
   And nod to the summer winds all the day long.
As blue is the sky, and as fair are the flowers,
   The earth is a wonderful picture outspread ;
But I turn from the sunlight, the songs, and the blossoms,
   And sigh for the beautiful days that are dead.

Afar o'er the hill-tops the day robed in splendor,
   Comes forth like a queen from the realm of the sun,
And the valleys uplift the white veil of their slumber
   To welcome the dawn of a day just begun.
The dew-spangled lawn and the glittering forest
   Drop gems at my feet and o'erjewel my head ;
But I long for the freshness and joy of the mornings
   That came with the beautiful days that are dead.

Oh sweet, vanished days that went out with the sunset,
   Shall I find ye alone in the land of my dreams—
With the friends, and the songs, and the flashes of glad-
      ness,
   And your skies mirrored fair on the silvery streams?

Shall the heart ever mourn for a song that is silent,
When sweetest of harmonies o'er it are shed?
Shall the dark buried past find no bright resurrection?
Shall eternity bring back the days that are dead?

THE SWEETEST HOUR.

I N the sweet closes of the summer days,
When golden clouds have changed to amethyst,
And silver stars gleam thro' the filmy haze
That night unfolds in shades of purple mist—
After the birds have ceased their vesper songs
And lullabies, above the unfledged nest ;
When twittering swallows seek the sheltering eaves,
And bright-winged insects flutter to their rest—

There comes the sweetest hour of all.the day,
When flowers unfold their fragrance on the air,
And choice perfumes are borne upon the breeze—
Nature's sweet incense and her silent prayer.
Blest hour, in which the vexing cares of earth
Roll like a burden from the weary breast,
And all the troubled waves of life are stilled,
As once the Saviour lulled the sea to rest.

In such an hour, how soothing to the heart
Are strains of music murmured soft and low,
Like waves that ripple on a summer sea
And break on golden sands in ebb and flow.

Blessed and holy hour when heaven is near
  And the glad soul mounts up on airy wing,
So near the gates of jasper and of pearl,
  We almost hear the song the angels sing.

And oh ! if angel visitants may come
  From out the shining spheres to this dull earth,
Or if the soul may antedate the hour
  And catch bright glimpses of its coming birth,
It must be when, with hearts attuned to love—
  The perfect love which casteth out all fear—
The earth grows dim to our far-seeing eyes,
  While heavenly strains float in upon the ear !

THE WINDOW OVER THE WAY.

THERE 'S a dainty window over the way,
     Draped with laces and decked with flowers,
Where a golden bird in a fairy cage
     Sings and swings through the daylight hours ;
But his voice has ever a mournful note,
     As if he sighed for an absent mate,
Or dreamed of the forest green and free
     Beyond the bars of his golden grate.

There 's a sweet, pale face, with heaven-blue eyes,
     That looks from the window over the way
With a wishful gaze at the far-off skies
     And the golden glow of the fading day.
And the snowy hands, with their golden rings,
     Are lifted often in vague unrest,
Lightly flitting from flower to flower,
     Or folded over the dainty breast.

And I wonder if under the silken robe,
     And flash of the shining golden chain,
The bird's sweet song with the mournful tone
     Wakens an echo akin to pain ;

For I know that many an aching heart
  Beats like the bird with prisoned wings ;
And I hear the sound of the grieving note
  In many a song that the poet sings.

And I long to open the gilded cage,
  And speed the happy bird as it flies,
And to hear the music of happy songs,
  Wherein no measure of sadness lies ;
And oft when the day is growing dim,
  To my heart I whisper, soft and low,
Would we were out of the reach of pain,
  Where the fadeless roses of heaven blow.

MY MISSING SHIPS.

I 'M waiting for my ships to come from sea ;
   They 're overdue by many a weary day ;
Richly freighted with the fairest hopes of life—
   Are they lost, or have they drifted far away?

One was filled with colors bright,
   Such as cunning artists blend
Into scenes of living light,
   Whose sweet witchery can lend
Enchantment to the humblest scene
   Wherein the pictures dwell ;
I fondly hoped my hand might learn
   To weave the witching spell.

One was full of glorious thoughts,
   Such as poets love to weave
Into chaplets rich and rare,
   Highest honors to achieve :
I hoped for power to weave the verse
   In patterns pure and bright—
To sway the listening multitudes
   And lead them toward the light.

And one rich bark was freighted
    With music's heavenly tone
To raise the soul from earthly things
    To regions of its own :
I craved the glorious gift of song
    To bear the soul on high,
Upon the waves of harmony
    Into the upper sky.

And one, the richest ship of all,
    Was filled with human love
For all things bright and beautiful—
    My unreturning dove.

And with a sad and doubting face
    I sit beside the sea,
And watch for but the floating wreck
    Of my rich argosy ;
Unheeding what the wild waves say,
    With ceaseless monotone—
" Thou waitest not beside the sea
    For sunken ships alone."

"LITTLE BOY BLUE."

D EAR little boy with the trowsers blue,
And eyes of the same bright sunny hue,
With hair the color of flaxen thread,
Curling in ringlets round your head,
" Blow up your horn."

Blow a blast on your tiny horn,
And frighten the sheep from the field of corn,
Scare the horses out of the hay,
And then you may go to your merry play ;
" The sheep are in the meadow."

The sheep came in through the open bars
And browsed all night by the light of the stars ;
They trampled the hay beneath their feet,
And fed on the meadow lilies sweet ;
" The cows are in the corn."

Brindle and Spot are in the corn,
They leaped the fence in the early morn,
And the silken tassels are bending low,
'Neath the onward march of the coming foe ;
" Where 's the little boy that looks after the sheep ? "

What has become of the little man
Who blows his horn like an infant Pan?
We need him here ; oh, where can he be?
Some one run to the meadow and see ;—
" Under the hay-stack, fast asleep."

Here on a fragrant bed of hay
The blue-eyed truant in slumber lay—
Dreaming of fields that need no bars,
And meadows spangled with golden stars.
And I say, dream on, my beautiful boy—
Dream of a world that is full of joy ;
Gather the rose-buds while you may,
And forget the sheep and the fields of hay.
All too soon will you watch and wait,
Guarding the fields by Mammon's gate,
And the world will trample our precious corn,
Tho' never so bravely you blow your ho;¬

SPRING GROVE.

OUT of the noisy city,
  The tramp of hurrying feet,
The whirl of a busy million,
  The dust of a crowded street ;
Safe from the din and conflict,
  Far from the noise and strife,
Lieth a beautiful city,
  With never a sound of life.

A city so fair that we almost dream
  We have reached the golden shore,
Where evermore we may walk in white,
  Where they "sorrow and sigh no more."
Where the sun with a mellowed splendor
  Throws shadows of softest hue ;
Where the wild bird's song is sweetest,
  And the sky of a deeper blue.

Beautiful, silent city !
  We left thee with lingering feet,
And a spirit filled with solemn awe,
  'Neath an influence calm and sweet ;

And ever in memory's chambers,
    The beautiful picture will dwell—
The lake in its sylvan beauty,
    The shady and tangled dell ;

The little grave that affection
    Hath hallowed with many a tear ;
The granite shaft, and the rustic cross,
    And the soldier's grave so dear.
And I thought when this restless life is o'er,
    How sweet it would be to rest
Where the good and brave are sleeping
    The sleep that remains for the blest.

AT REST.

ALL thro' the beautiful summer,
    Her path led down to the way
Where she entered the valley of shadows
    That leads to eternal day ;
And ere the splendor of autumn
    Had waned to days that were chill,
The clasp of her hand was loosened,
    And the lovely voice was still.

And we who had watched her fading
    So peacefully, day by day,
Could scarcely weep when the spirit
    Escaped from its house of clay ;
For she feared not the way of darkness.
    As she said with her latest breath :
"Yea, tho' I walk thro' the valley,
    I fear not the shadow of death."

And thus, with a faith confiding,
    She leaned on her Savior's breast.
And calmly, as one in slumber,
    She entered the heavenly rest.

And we felt in the Sabbath stillness
  Which fell on the darkened room
Where she lay in her fair young beauty.
  There was nothing there of gloom :

For the hands of love had decked her—
  The beautiful bride of death—
With fair white roses and heliotropes,
  That filled the room with their breath.
And we felt, though the sainted spirit
  Had flown to its home on high,
She had left in our hearts a memory
  Whose fragrance can never die.

IN MEMORIAM.

How shall we twine the Christmas green,
   Or wreath the Easter lilies white,
Or find a voice for happy hymns,
   When Sabbaths dawn in radiant light.

Our human hearts with grief are dumb,
   We grope thro' mists of blinding tears:
The while we know she waits for us,
   Beyond the swiftly whirling years.

A glorious advent day was hers:
   While all the earth was robed in white
She put the robes immortal on,
   To dwell where morning has no night.

And even while our aching hearts
   In grief and bitter anguish swell,
Refusing to be comforted,
   We know, with her, that all is well.

But oh! we miss the loving voice,
   The step in each familiar spot;
Our hearts send up the Rachel cry—
   We mourn because the loved is not.

LAMENT FOR ALICE CAREY.

OH, sweet wild flowers of early spring!
  Pale hyacinth, and daffodil,
And blue-eyed violet, tender thing,
  Growing beside the shady rill;
Sweet pansy, with the look of thought,
  And lily of the valley fair,
Bend low your heads, with sorrow fraught,
  And looks of softest sadness wear:
For she who loved you best below,
  Hath no more need of earthly flowers;
Now, where the bright immortelles grow,
  She can not miss a love like ours.

Fair meadows, shining in the sun,
  And forest, dark with mistletoe,
Bright rivers, flowing swiftly down,
  Laughing and rippling as ye go—
No more will you appear more bright,
  In the sweet sunshine of her love,
As by the rivers of delight,
  Through pastures green, her steps now rove.

Sad hearts that ache for sympathy,
  Bruised reeds bent by life's stormy wind.
The tenderest heart that beats for you
  No more the broken chords may bind.
And in the blossom-laden air
  I seem to hear a sad refrain,
A low and thrilling monotone
  Of " Never more on earth again."

RELEASED.

WITH patient feet she walked life's weary way,
With patient hands she wrought her homely toil,
And kept thro' all her dreary pilgrimage
A pure unselfish soul, without a soil.

There was no halo round about her head
Such as the pictured saints of Raphael wear.
And yet a radiance lit the wondrous eyes
And rested softly on her brow and hair.

And there was something in the mournful lips
That touched your sympathy to sudden tears.
That one should carry such a weight of grief
Whose life had numbered but a few brief years.

She had an artist's eye for all things fair.
A poet's soul for all the pure and bright :
The sunset sky a language had for her.
And lovely visions dawned upon her sight.

A love for all the beautiful in art.
A dream of glorious lands beyond the sea :
Yet, mute and uncomplaining of her lot,
She bore the heavy burdens cheerfully.

And music, too, found echo in her soul
   That throbbed and trembled 'neath sweet melody ;
A sad and prisoned song her spirit sung,
   Even as the shell sings of the far-off sea.

Therefore, I did not weep when others wept,
   To see the hands crossed o'er the pulseless breast,
And the sweet eyes closed in a dreamless sleep,
   The weary feet forever more at rest.

I knew that she had fought the winning fight,
   And conquered self, and put beneath her feet
The world with all its vanity and strife,
   Ambition's siren song, and love so sweet.

I knew the brow, so free from mortal sin,
   Was crowned at last with fadeless immortelle,
And that the crowning angel had removed
   Forever more the gloomy asphodel.

NETTIE.

‘ THOU gavest her, dear Lord, into our keeping,
       And Thou hast called her home.
With breaking hearts we strive to dry our weeping,
   And say, " Thy will be done."
We know full well our bud of brightest promise
   Will blossom in the radiant summer-land,
And the sweet voice that filled our home with music
   Now mingles with the glorious angel band.
We know that safe above the cares and sorrows
   And wails of earthly woe, she is at rest,
And that the cup which Thou hast drank, our Father,
   Thou knowest for us is best.

Our dear, lost Nettie, life is very lonely ;
   We know not how to pass the weary day :
Thro' all the house we miss thy joyous footstep,
   Thy light and merry play ;
And when at morn we miss thy tender greeting,
   Thy kiss at night, and see thine empty bed,
We can not still the heart's tumultuous beating,
   And know that thou art dead.

Oh ! was there ever sorrow like to ours?
Can anguish ever take a form more wild,
Than that which sweeps upon us when we miss
From out our home a loved and only child?

NEVER AGAIN.

A MONG the words full fraught with deepest meaning,
 That sweep the soul with bitterness and pain,
None bear the echoes of all tender sorrow
 Like to these simple words—" Never again."

Never again for us the sweet June roses
 Will hold the fragrance that they held of yore ;
The warm south winds can bring the bloom and freshness,
 The budding joy of spring, to us no more.

The sky may wear its tint of softest azure,
 Yet under all we hear the sad refrain,
For days that faded with the golden sunset,
 Whose light shall never shine for us again.

And bending over pale and silent faces
 We drop our bitter, unavailing tears ;
Weeping because the voice of sweetest music
 Shall sound no more thro' all life's weary years.

We hoard the withered flower and tear-stained letter,
 The little shoe that pattered on the floor,
The curl of glossy hair, the faded garment
 That once the darling of the household wore.

No freshly gathered rose could hold the meaning
　We read amid these faded leaves of ours ;
No fair white page, tho' traced with golden letters,
　Could bring such memories of happy hours.

So hiding from the world our priceless treasure,
　And locking in our hearts their secret pain,
We weep above the fragments of our idols,
　Knowing our sorrows and our tears are vain.

THE VESPER BELL.

MOURNFUL bell, in the steeple high,
Dropping your chimes on the evening sky,

Ever ringing a dead day's knell
At the vesper hour, oh solemn bell!

Tho' I know your sound is a call to prayer
Wafted out on the summer air,

Calling the weary wanderer in
From the dust of toil and the stain of sin,

Saying, in silvery waves of sound,
Seek for rest while it may be found;

Tho' I know how the burden of sin and care
Is rolled away by the breath of prayer.

And the hope which dawns with a happier thrill
When the angel whispers, " Peace, be still."

Ever there comes with the vesper bell
A sadness beyond my words to tell—

A backward glimpse of the whirling years,
And a blindness born of sudden tears:

Not for the days which lie behind,
Gone like the viewless, rushing wind ;

Not for the graves of buried hopes,
That lie so thickly on all the slopes ;

But once, when the day was going down
Like a dying king, in robe and crown,

And the bell was ringing the vesper chime
For one day less on the shore of time,

A life went out on the unknown sea
That breaks on the shores of eternity—

A beautiful spirit passed away
Where night shall never darken the day.

And ever I feel the solemn spell
When I hear the chimes of the evening bell ;

For it seems the voice of the spirit fled,
And a presence comes with soundless tread,

And rolls away the burden of years,
And I see her face through the mist of tears.

UNRETURNING.

THE sands were white in the morning sun,
    And the sea-birds sailed on level wing,
The waves came dancing in to the beach
    Where boats were rocking with lazy swing.
And a ship sailed out till, dim and white,
The sails went down from my aching sight.

And what cared I for the shining sands
    Or the merry songs that the sailors sung,
When my heart was full of passionate pain,
    And my soul with the parting sorrow wrung?
For the world grew strangely dark to me
When the ship went out on the widening sea.

And the years went on, the tides came in.
    The white sands shifted along the shore,
And the sea-birds skimmed o'er the sunken reef,
    But the ship that sailed came home no more,
And the broken wrecks come drifting back
From the desolate course of her outward track.

MOTHER GOOSE.

"TELL me a story, mamma,
    One that is not very long.
I am getting so tired and sleepy,
    Or sing me a little song ;
Something about the boy in blue
    That watches the cows and sheep.
Who ought to get up and blow the horn,
    But he lies in the hay asleep."

And I answered with quick impatience,
    While he hung his sleepy head :
"No, not a story or song to-night :
    Bertie must go to bed."
But after the room was silent,
    And the weary boy asleep,
And never a sound fell on my ear,
    Save the cricket's lonely peep,

The voice, with the tone of pleading,
    Kept coming, again and again,
"Tell me a story, or sing me a song,"
    Till I could not bear the pain ;

So I went with stealthy footstep
  To see how my darling slept—
Weak and foolish though it may seem,
  I knelt by the bed and wept.

To think that I had denied him
  The song that he loved so well,
And refused the simple story,
  That none but a mother can tell.
And I said, " Sleep on, sweet dreamer ;
  Fear not the cows and the sheep ;
Dream that you lie in the meadow,
  Under the hay asleep.
All too soon will you waken,
  To watch o'er the fields of corn ;
All too soon will the sheep get in,
  Though you bravely blow your horn."

A SUMMER STORM.

L OW in the west a leaden bank uprising
Shuts out the radiant blue, and dims the sun,
While hosts of tiny clouds, like flying banners,
Mingle their many colors into one ;
And rolling heavily, like roar of battle,
The thunders sweep along the dismal sky,
While gathering shadows dim the field and forest,
And wandering song-birds to their shelter fly.

A flash, as if the doors of heaven were opened,
And fiery writing blazoned on the wall ;
Then heavier darkness, and a solemn grandeur,
As if a dead world slept beneath a pall.
A mournful whisper creeps along the valley,
The forest lightens with its upturned leaves,
And far across the meadow, from her covert,
The mourning dove in plaintive accent grieves.

A swaying of the forest, like the bending
Of loyal subjects when their king is nigh ;
A fiery flame, swift followed by the thunder,
Like charges where a thousand heroes die.

Anon, a rift of blue thro' broken shadows
  Shines where the stormy rack its way pursued ;
Then, arching over earth, the radiant promise
  In beauty and in glory is renewed.

DRIFTING WITH THE TIDE.

EVEN as the rower in the waters calm
    Lets drop the oars, to drift with the slow tide,
And listens dreamily to far-off sounds—
    Listens with hands dropped idly by his side,
And hears, perchance, the music of a flute
    Come trembling o'er the silvery summer sea.
Or chime of distant bells, borne on the air,
    Breaking in throbs of mournful melody—

And sees, as in a waking dream, the sails
    Of the white ships pass slowly from his view,
And the round moon come up above the wave,
    Silvering a path across the waters blue ;
Or the bright stars in clustering groups of light,
    Like gems upon the brow of some fair queen,
Mirrored upon the waters clear and bright,
    Like the enchantment of some gorgeous scene ;

So am I drifting, idly with the tide,
    Weary with rowing through the rapid waves.
Where whirling waters threatened to engulph,
    And draw me down to deep and dismal caves.

'Gainst wind and wave I gained this quiet rest.
And with calm heart I watch the fading sails.
For me the storms are past, the tempest stilled,
I fear no more the fury of the gales.

And memory bells are ringing in my ear
Sweet sounds from the dim shores of long ago—
The dim and flowery shores from which I sailed
When earth was radiant with the morning's glow.
Alas! the flowers vanished from my view,
For the broad stream grew far from shore to shore,
And all the glory faded from the skies,
And tempest-clouds above my track did lower.

But now, with childish trustfulness, I wait
All patiently, beneath the dews of even,
The pilot boatman that shall guide me hence,
Out of the twilight, to a glorious haven.
And I shall see once more the flowery banks
From which my bark went forth upon the stream ;
And in the perfect rapture of repose,
The stormy past will vanish as a dream.

"THE WAY OF THE WORLD."

THERE are beautiful songs that we never sing,
And names that are never spoken ;
There are treasures guarded with jealous care,
And kept as a sacred token :
There are faded flowers, and letters dim
With tears that have rained above them
For the fickle words and the faithless hearts
That taught us how to love them.

There are sighs that come in our joyous hours,
To chasten our dreams of gladness,
And tears that spring to our aching eyes
In moments of thoughtful sadness :
For the blithest bird that sings in spring
Will flit with the waning summer,
And lips that we kissed in fondest love
Will smile on the first new comer.

Over the breast where lilies rest
In white hands, stilled forever.
The roses of June will nod and blow
Unheeding the hearts that sever ;

And lips that quiver in silent grief.
All words of hope refusing;
Will lightly turn to the fleeting joys
That perish with the using.

Summer blossoms and winter snows,
Love and its sweet elysian,
Hope, like a siren dim and fair,
Quickening our fainting vision ;
Drooping spirit and failing pulse,
Where untold memories hover ;
Eyelids touched with the seal of death—
And the fitful dream is over.

UNDER THE AUTUMN RAIN.

M Y heart is full of sadness to-night
    As I hear the sound of the falling rain,
And thronging memories fill my soul
    With a feeling akin to pain ;
For I see in fancy the smiling eyes,
    But wait for the steps in vain,
And I weep, that the lips which smiled in May
    Are under the autumn rain.

For the summer is past, and the harvest
    Is gathered in from the storm,
And the robin has flown from the roof-tree
    To skies that are ever warm ;
And the leaves have dropped from the roses,
    And the hands that we loved are still,
Never to gather the summer flowers,
    Our favorite vase to fill.

Though we know in the beautiful city
    Our loved ones are gathered home,
Sheltered for aye, from the chilling blast,
    Where sorrow may never come,

Yet our hearts are forever aching
  And crying in vain, in vain,
For the eyes that shone in the May time,
  Shut close 'neath the autumn rain.

SORROW CROWNED.

OH, idle hands that lie content
    In idleness the livelong day,
And lips that never, never smile,
    And eyes that look so far away,
Think you I know not why the hands
    Drop wearied from their task apart.
And why the sunlight of a smile
    Can wake no answer in thy heart?

I know there's not a gentle song,
    Sung lowly at the hush of eve,
But wakes in thee some memory,
    And makes the sorrowing spirit grieve :
And when the earth is all athrob
    With pulses of the living spring,
And troops of silver clouds float by
    Like happy spirits wandering ;

When earth is one grand psalm of praise
    And tribute to the bounteous Giver,
And life goes on thro' flowery ways,
    As thro' bright banks some shining river—

The sunshine only mocks thy grief
  That never more from joy can borrow
One moment of forgetfulness,
  Or hope for any coming morrow.

ONLY.

ONLY a kiss at parting,
  Only a fond embrace ;
But the tide of years, with its hopes and fears,
  Can never the dream efface.

Only a careless meeting,
  Only a chilling gaze ;
But the heart will carry the cruel wound
  Through all life's devious ways.

Only a bitter heartache,
  Only some womanly tears ;
But the love that changes not with change
  Lives on thro' eternity's years.

Only the thrilling memory
  Of a happy moment fled,
And all the days that follow its wake
  Are cold, and empty, and dead.

TEARS.

A YE, tears that well up from the heart's deep foun-
    tain,
  The while my feet press through the rustling leaves
Of autumn fields, shorn of the golden grain,
  Conscious that I am bearing in no sheaves.

With empty hands I come too late for gleaning,
  The harvest gathered, and the vintage pressed ;
I lingered where the wayside flowers were blooming,
  And idly sought green lanes of pleasant rest.

And now, through fields of sharp and bristling stubble
  My weary feet have lost their wonted power,
Take Thou my empty hands, O pitying Savior,
  Even though I come beyond the eleventh hour.

A JUNE IDYL.

JUST far enough from the dim town
    To see the spires gleam through the haze,
And catch the glory of the sun
    That gilds them with a golden blaze.
How sweet, in such a day as this,
    To watch through interlacing trees
The troops of silver clouds go by,
    Blown softly by a summer breeze,
That scarcely lifts from off my brow
    The locks which fall in loosened maze,
Abandoned to the winds that blow,
    This sweetest of all summer days !

Between the sunset glow and I,
    I see the billowy fields of grain
Lie half in sunshine, half in shade,
    As o'er our lives fall joy and pain ;
And far away I see the hills
    Traced dimly on the evening sky,
Like blessed isles in happy dreams,
    Where all our golden treasures lie.

And softly on the charmed repose
 There falls a far-off evening bell,
A sound that drops from out the sky,
 For the lost day a dying knell.
Float calmly through the sunset gate,
 While earth and sky are all in tune?
Farewell ! thou rare and perfect day,
 Sweetest of all the days of June.

The happy, twittering birds return,
 To sing above the unfledged nest,
And bright-winged insects quit the sky,
 And flutter to their evening rest.
Afar from all life's jarring sounds,
 Alone with nature and with God,
My heart sends up a happy song,
 The while my tears bedew the sod.
If to my life's brief term of years
 I might from out the banished past
Have one bright day to live again,
 I 'd choose the hour that vanished last.

A DAY IN THE WOODS.

W̲E walked through the grand old forest,
       O'er drifts of withering leaves,
And through the fields where the harvest
    Was gathered in shining sheaves;
The sun was high in the heavens,
    Veiled with a luminous mist,
And the clouds kept changing from amber gold
    To opal and amethyst.

The oak wore royal purple,
    The beech was in cloth of gold,
The elm and hickory flecked with green,
    The maple in scarlet bold;
Over the shining river
    There floated an azure haze,
And the hills seemed fading away like dreams
    That we knew in the far-off days.

A brooding stillness was over all,
    And many an empty nest
Where late the garrulous mother-bird
    Had warbled her young to rest;

And a silence fell between us,
    A feeling too deep for words,
As we thought of the vanished summer,
    And the empty nests of the birds.

I gathered the maple's scarlet leaves
    That floated and fell at my feet,   .
Content to walk in the silence,
    Feeling a joy complete ;
And out of the autumn forest
    With thoughtful hearts we came,
When the sun was low in the western sky,
    Bathed in a crimson flame.

Our paths lay not together,
    We parted at eventide ;
I knew that the beautiful day was dead,
    And something I knew beside.
I knew that the vanished summer
    No memory held for me
So sweet as the bright October day,
    When I walked in the woods with thee.

A SUMMER NIGHT.

THE drowsy air of the summer night
   Is stirred by the song of the katydid ;
Under a canopy of leaves
   The wings of the humming-bird are hid ;
Out of the heart of the mignonette
   A fragrance floats on the passing air.
And the signal lamps are hung on high
   To lead our souls from a world of care.

The tremulous sound of a plaintive tune
   Blown soft and low from a distant flute,
And the far-off tinkle of rhythmic keys
   Are mingled sweet as a chiming lute ;
The vesper songs of the birds are still,
   The lily cradles the slumbering bee,
The hush of twilight covers the earth,
   And darkness gathers over the sea.

And I wonder where is the vanished day
   That went like a king through gates of gold,
With the dewy robe of the evening mist
   Trailing in many a shining fold.

I know that the morrow waits, perchance,
    To gladden my way with summer flowers ;
But where is the beautiful yesterday,
    With its shining train of sunny hours?

Does some one wait in the happy light
    Of the summer day that is dead to me?
Will some glad message follow the sun
    To brighten the day that is yet to be?
Beyond the feverish dreams of life
    Shall we find, when the fitful hour is o'er,
The garnered hopes of a happy past
    In the golden light of the farther shore?

HOME TO THE VILLAGE.

SO you have been to the village
And the homestead over the hill,
And walked once more down the shady road
  That leads to the old grist-mill?
What of the old log school-house,
  With its benches narrow and hard,
The desks where we used to carve our names,
  And the trees that shaded the yard?

The homestead roof is mossy and gray,
  Its rooms are empty and still,
The weeds are trailing over the walks,
  And mildew darkens the sill.
The dear old road by the river
  Is tracked by the iron rail,
And the shadows under the maples
  Have fled as a swift-told tale.
The school-house, ragged and roofless,
  Stands where it did of yore;
But the dancing feet of the children
  Waken the echoes no more.

Alas! for the dear old school-house—
  But where are the boys and girls,
With their merry pranks and laughter,
  Their songs and their sunny curls?
Is the old shop-door still open?
  Does the anvil chorus ring
To the strokes of the sturdy blacksmith,
  And the songs that he used to sing?
And the quiet spot on the hillside,
  Where the sweet blush roses grow—
Did you look on the shining marbles
  For the names that we used to know?

Where are the boys and girls? Ah, me!
  I talked with a gray-haired man,
Never guessing, until he told,
  That he was the merry Dan
Who locked the master out in the cold
  And made him treat the crowd;
Who stood up longest at spelling-school,
  And looked so handsome and proud.
There's a grand new school-house on the spot
  Where the anvil used to sound,
And the arm that wielded the heavy sledge
  Is resting under the ground.

I walked where the western sunbeams
Touched with their fingers of gold
The names on the mossy marbles
That we loved in the days of old.
And the purple shadows of evening
Fell on the day and my tears,
As I wept for the vanished faces
That I knew in the bygone years.
They are gone, and their names are fading;
They are scattered far and near.
Some have carved on the scroll of fame
The names that were first carved here;
But oft, in the din and jostle,
There cometh a vision still
Of the beautiful vanished summers
And the school-house over the hill.

A SONG OF VANISHED YEARS.

I HAVE within my heart a song,
 Perhaps 't were better left unsung ;
Its sadness might oppress some soul
 E'en as mine own with grief is wrung.
But sometimes when the day grows dim,
 And none are by to heed my tears,
I touch the harp of memory,
 And sing the song of vanished years.

I sing of one who, years ago,
 Looked at the world with eager eyes,
And longings for the far-off goal
 That seemed so fair and rich a prize ;
Of one whose locks were sunny brown,
 Whose eyes were all undimmed by tears,
Whose heart kept time to sweetest songs,
 A rhythm of hope that drowned the fears.

Whose voice had learned no sad refrain,
 Whose heart had felt no shade of care,
Whose soul had known no blight of sin,
 Yet lowly dwelt in humble prayer.

The simple maiden, daisy-crowned,
    Dreamed of a fadeless wreath of bay,
Longed for a Poet's fame, and sighed
    To sing some grand undying lay.

She knew not of the thorny paths
    O'er which her weary feet must climb
To reach the sun-crowned home of thought,
    And win the coronal sublime.
She journeyed on with patient feet,
    O'er many a long and weary way,
Stooping to gather way-side flowers
    Whose sweetness cheered the summer day.

Sometimes, along the toilsome road
    She gladdened, with her daisy chain,
Some weary pilgrim bowed with grief,
    And charmed his heart away from pain.
But ever as she gained some steep
    The Temple seemed more dim and far,
And fading from her aching eyes
    As from the morn recedes the star.

Until with hope too long deferred,
    And many an idol turned to clay,
Her heart grew sick of all its dream,
    Her feet grew weary of the way.

And holding in her failing hand
  The flowers she gathered for a crown,
Her bright ambitions, one by one
  A sacrifice she laid them down.

And looking back across the years
  With eyes no longer filled with light,
She saw once more the meadows green,
  The cowslips and the lilies bright ;
And on her brow, where silver threads
  Outnumbered far the threads of brown,
She only prayed to wear once more
  Her childhood's faith and daisy crown.

She only longed to sing once more,
  Some childish song of love and trust,
Forgetting all the golden fruit
  Whose taste was only bitter dust.
Forgetting the loud trumpet blare
  Of fame, whose echo dies away,
She learned too late, that valley flowers
  Were sweeter than the crown of bay.

TO IRENE.

SWEET friend beside the sunset sea
    Whose waters kiss the golden shore,
My thoughts thro' all the livelong day
    Have been within the past once more.
And tho' I walk 'mid winter snows,
    While thou art in a summer clime,
In memory I have lived again
    The sweetness of a vanished time.

The glory of a day in June,
    A long and perfect summer day—
That glided out to meet the moon
    In full orbed splendor on her way;
And when the solemn hush of eve
    Fell round us like the soul of prayer,
Your voice in sweetest cadence broke
    The stillness of the summer air.

" Ave Marie " was the hymn
    You sang, while daylight fainter grew,
And one by one the stars came out
    Like sentries on the field of blue;

And something in the tender strain
  Called from my heart a flood of tears,
And stirred the depths of memory
  To pulses of long vanished years.

Sweet friend beside the sunset sea,
  I know not if on earth again
Thy voice of song shall thrill my soul,
  And charm away its bitter pain ;
But if there be a summer land
  Where happy days go on forever,
I 'll clasp once more thy loving hand
  Where parting words no more shall sever.

RECOMPENSE.

I READ to-day a sweet, impassioned sonnet,
   As Shakespeare ever sang his chosen love ;
And while my brimming eyes dwelt long upon it,
   My wayward thoughts forbidden paths did rove.
I wished that time might roll his chariot backward,
   And give once more the bright, brief days of youth,
That I might once inspire such passionate numbers
   And prove beyond a doubt man's love and truth.

I know such idle dreaming ill becomes me,
   Who stand midway upon the slope of time ;
Bnt flowers have blossomed lately in my pathway
   That never budded in my youth's brief prime.
If life's strange book, its leaves one-half turned over,
   Show me a fairer page than all the rest,
I know not how the mystery to discover—
   Shall I tear out the leaf that seems the best?

'T is said that when the lingering blasts of winter
   Cut off the spring and chill the early flowers,
The summer burns in still more gorgeous splendor
   To compensate for all the missing hours ;

That if the day in rain and stormy sobbing,
Like tears of passion, wear the hours away,
The sunset glow sets all the earth a-throbbing,
And joy fills up the measure of the day.

It may be that the feet, so tired of climbing,
Have reached the station looking out each way,
Where I may hear afar the joyful chiming
Of bells that usher in the perfect day ;
And looking back o'er days of sad heart-aching,
Count all my griefs as nothing to the gain,
And looking forward, where the light is breaking,
Thank God that pleasure cometh after pain.

"TRUSTING IN THEE."

SOFTLY above the silent camp
   The stars shone out in midnight glory,
Repeating through the shining spheres
   The music of the wondrous story.

And in my heart a sweet refrain
   Through all my waking hours kept ringing,
The anthem of a soul at rest—
   A soul that could not cease from singing.

And when the golden morning broke
   Above the tents so white and shining,
My heart went up to meet the day
   Beyond the reach of all repining.

And with the dawn my waking voice
   Rose in an anthem glad and free,
The song I sang at eventide,
   " Still I am trusting, Lord, in thee."

ROSEMARY.

" 'T is for remembrance."—*Shakespeare.*

ONLY a little green and bitter spray
    Of fading leaves I give into thy keeping—
A bunch of rosemary, chilled by the frost,
    And withered by the tears my eyes are weeping.
" 'T is for remembrance, love ! " oh, pray remember
    Our spring-time wanderings and our summer days !
When you were all my world, and I was happy
    In winning from the world my meed of praise.

There 's not a path which we have walked together
    But seems a hallowed spot for evermore ;
There 's not a page whereon thine eyes have rested,
    But I have learned its lessons o'er and o'er ;
There 's not an hour, however dark and dreary,
    But hope revives with memories of thee.
Then take this rosemary, 't is for remembrance,
    And oh, I pray you, love, remember me !

I left the heart's-ease and the purple pansy
    To fade and wither under wintry skies ;
I could not wear the one or bear the other,
    So much of thought was in its honest eyes.

But from my garden bed this little spray
I rescue from the pitiless November,
And bid you wear it for the thought it brings—
Wear it for me, and oh, I pray, remember!

THE FORGOTTEN SONG.

DEAR friend, have you forgotten the day
 When the haze hung low o'er the river,
And out of the autumn sunset sky
Came flashes of crimson and purple dye,
 Like arrows shot from a golden quiver?

And softly over the fading fields
 We heard the partridge calling,
And you sang the sweetest of songs to me,
As we stood together beneath the tree
 And watched the red leaves falling.

What was the burden of that sweet song?
 I wonder if you remember.
'T was a song of a love no change could move,
Of friendship that only time could prove,
 The same from May to December.

The leaves came down, and the sky grew cold,
 And the song-birds sought their cover,
And you forgot the words of the song
When the winter eves grew chill and long,
 And the summer of love was over.

Oh, golden day that drifted away
With the haze of the shining river !
And the partridge call, and sweetest of all,
The song, as I watched the red leaves fall—
I shall dream of the day forever.

OLD LETTERS.

O NLY a bundle of yellow letters,
 Faded, wrinkled, and torn,
Tied with a ribbon that once was blue,
 In the time of my girlhood worn ;
And yet they bring before my gaze
 The faces of long ago,
Some that lie 'neath the waving grass,
 And the winter's drifting snow.

And one by one the days come back,
 When I opened with eager hand,
And a throbbing heart that was full of joy,
 To hear from a distant land.
They breathed of friendship, true and warm,
 And a love that could not change ;
I read them now like one in a dream,
 They seem so old and strange.

It seems so very long ago,
 Since I was the happy girl,
Who sent in my letters sweet wild flowers
 And sometimes a glossy curl.

And oft in the forest green and wide,
'Neath some broad spreading tree,
With the song of the wild bird overhead,
I carolled as wild and free.

Now I can trace a silver thread
In the hair that was once so brown,
And the dear old forest seems so far
From the heart of the busy town.
The bird is caged that sings to me now,
And beats his prisoned wings ;
There seems a sad and weary plaint,
In every song that he sings.
And oft, when wearied with many cares,
To my soul I whisper low,
Would that the bird and I were free,
To fly where the winds might blow.

LIFE'S AUTUMN.

NOT for pale cheeks and fading hair
     Do love's delicious roses grow,
Nor sudden raptures wake the pulse
     Whose tides have ceased to ebb and flow.
The sad, cold heights of middle age
     Are barren of all wild delights,
The days seem only whitely set
     To mark a place between the nights.
Slow pulses tuned to dropping tears,
     Like autumn rains that fall so chill,
When all the summer flowers are dead
     And field and forest brown and still.

Some sweet regrets for vanished youth,
     Some fragrant leaves, slow pressed by pain,
We treasure from the wasted time
     Whose sands we may not turn again.
Behind us, lying dim and fair,
     The valley of our youth appears,
Warm with the light of memory,
     Seen thro' the sad, regretful tears.

Before us, stretching chill and far,
   The future, dim and undefined,
Lies like the somber shadow-side
   Of all the sunshine left behind.
Beside the lonely, fireless hearth
   We watch the ashes, cold and gray,
Whose happy fires burned dim and low,
   And faded with the yesterday.

ONE DAY IN MAY.

DIM was the woodland and fair was the weather,
   And blue were the skies of the beautiful May,
When laughing and singing we wandered together
   With hearts attuned to the happy day.
We sought the shade where the birds were singing
   And busily building the summer nest,
Where the branches, ever swaying and swinging,
   Should rock the twittering brood to rest.

The leaves of the forest were green and tender,
   The grass was velvet under our feet,
And tropical ferns in graceful splendor
   Drooped over violets dewy and sweet.
And the brook, released from its wintry prison,
   Sang o'er the pebbles and laughed along ;
And the meadow-lilies, newly risen,
   Drank in the joy of the happy song.

The earth was a psalm of love and beauty,
   Because of the birds and the budding flowers ;
And it seemed to us but a happy duty
   To linger there in the golden hours.

And never till life and its dreams are over,
And the sun has set on my latest day,
Shall fade from my heart the face of my lover,
Or the words that he said, that day in May.

A YEAR AND A DAY.

M Y beautiful May
    'T is a year and a day
Since my love and I went out together,
    With hearts as light
    As the day was bright,
And hand in hand in the sweet spring weather.

    We lingered over
    The scented clover
And watched the barge on the lazy stream,
    Till the golden day
    Had melted away
And left us dreaming a blissful dream.

    A year and a day
    Since the morn in May
When the apple-blossoms in snowy shower
    Fell like a rain
    In the sunny lane,
Leaving the fruit instead of the flower.

    My tears fall fast
    For the vanished past,

For blossom and fruit that fell together,
And the May-day dream
Like the fleeting gleam
Of a sunny sky in April weather.

I shall walk no more
By the river's shore
In the golden glow of the May's completeness,
For my love is dead,
And over his head
I will drop the flowers that he loved for sweetness.

Violets blue
That are tender and true,
Buds of lilies and snowy daisies,
And pansies rare
· Beyond all compare
For the thoughts they bring of his once sweet praises.

"UNDER THE MISTLETOE."

WILL you take the hand that I offer
    In fullest friendship to-day?
Letting " the dead past bury its dead,"
    Hiding the ashes away,
Looking beyond the changes
    That compass our years below,
Will you pledge your faith for eternity
    " Under the mistletoe?"

The years of time are too fleeting,
    The pulses of life too fast;
The roses wither so swiftly,
    The summers too soon are past:
And human words are but feeble
    To clothe deep feelings of love
As fathomless as the ocean deeps,
    As true as the stars above.

Nay, doubt not the motive or meaning,
    Life's sorrows have melted the dross;
The friendship I give is purest gold
    Won from its baser loss.

Pearls from a perilous diving
    Shine with no purer glow
Than the faith I offer you here to-day,
    " Under the mistletoe."

Will you take the hand that I offer,
    Holding it firm and fast,
Veiling the faults and the follies
    That dimmed the days of the past?
Let me not wait for an answer
    For a hope deferred is woe ;
But give me a loving greeting
    " Under the mistletoe."

THE LETTER.

B REAK into beautiful blossoms
    O buds of the sunny May,
And sing, my robin and bluebird,
    Your sweetest carol to-day—
For my love has written a letter,
    And the world is all in tune—
He is coming along with the roses
    In the fairest days of June.

I am counting the days between us—
    I am counting the moments and hours,
Telling my beads, like a solemn nun,
    On a rosary of flowers ;
For he said, when the buds of the roses
    Are flushing in royal red,
He is coming to claim a promise.
    (I wonder what I have said.)

Break into songs and blossoms,
    O birds and buds of spring ;
Lilies, scatter your fragrance,
    And sweetest song-birds, sing ;

And skies, drop golden sunshine
On the beautiful days of June,
For my love is coming to see me,
And the world is all in tune.

DECORATION ODE.

Air— *America*.

WITH reverent steps we come
To gather 'round their tomb,
The honored brave!
Those whom we loved so well
Who nobly fought and fell,
Foul treason's strife to quell,
Our land to save.

Bright wreaths and flowers we bring,
Fair offerings of the spring,
Their graves to strew,
While silent tear-drops well
From hearts that throb and swell,
As fame their deeds shall tell,
Those souls so true.

Fair children clothed in white,
Emblems of angels bright,
Are hither led!
And still, from year to year,
Shall pilgrims journey here,
And many a holy tear
Shall here be shed.

Oh God ! to Thee we raise
Our songs of highest praise
    For blessings past !
Make ùs still more revere
Their names who slumber here,
And guard our land so dear,
    While time shall last !

THE LOST SHIP.

O VER the roar of the signal gun
    The surging billows swept ;
Over the peaceful dreaming forms
    The treacherous waters crept ;
And the midnight sky, like a funeral pall,
    Hung low o'er the sinking ship,
And the cry of terror, " We 're lost, we 're lost ! "
    Went trembling from lip to lip.

Lost in the depths of the sounding sea,
    So near to the fair green shore,—
Whelmed 'neath the main's immensity,
    To return—ah, never more !
Lost while dreaming of " home, sweet home,"
    And the loved ones gathered there,
With never a kiss of fond farewell
    Nor time for a dying prayer.

Lost in the depths of the moaning sea,
    Lover and husband and friend,
Kindred seeking a free-born shore,
    Wanderer his journey to end ;

And ever the sorrowing cry goes up
    From hearts whence hope has fled,
" I shall see the face that I loved no more
    Till the sea gives up its dead."

PANSIES.

PANSY, born in the royal purple,
Linked by a subtle chain to thought,
Read me the spell of the mystic meaning
Deep in your chalice of gold inwrought.

Ages ago you were not a flower,
Such as I hold in my hand to-night,
But a soul a-thrill to love's sweet power,
Trembling under the spell of its might.

You saw how faithless was human passion,
Dew in the sunlight as swiftly fled,
And you left the guise of your earthly prison
And into the soul of the pansy sped.

Pansy, born in the royal purple,
Say, have I read your story aright?
What do you read in me that you tremble—
Hiding away in sudden fright?

Saw you, under my calm-eyed gazing,
Something I've hidden from all beside?
Keep my secret, O thoughtful flower—
Tell not the daisy close by your side.

Tell not the rose that is bending to listen,
Tell not the passion flower over your head,
That my heart is trembling to love's sweet music ;
Oh pansy, tell not a word that I 've said.

Fold my secret close in your bosom,
You who have learned that love is vain,
And in your crucible, deep and golden,
Charm my heart from its bitter pain.

"THE BEAUTIFUL SNOW."

WHAT we know of the beautiful snow
    This season, would fill a volume or so.
Pelting and melting, on pavement and sill ;
Blowing thro' crannies, ghostly and chill ;
Tracked thro' the house on the school-boy's boot—
Mixed with a portion of inky soot ;
Keeping the yard and house in a muss,
And stirring up many a family fuss.
      Oh, the snow, the terrible snow,
      Won't we rejoice when we see it go !

Who cares a fig who first wrote the poem ?
" Watson or Faxon," we do n't want to know him ;
He never stood with a brandishing broom,
Brushing out snow that was tracked in the room.
He never had little boys come from school,
Or he never had written himself such a fool ;
Praising and lauding the flakes as they fell,
Helping the gutters and rivers to swell.
      Oh, the snow, the terrible snow,
      Won't we rejoice when we see it go !

A LOST DAY.

A LL day I heard the merry Christmas bells
     Throbbing upon the chill and wintry air,
The while, with folded hands and silent lips,
   My heart was heavy with unanswered prayer.
All day beside my casement, mute and still,
   I waited with an eager, list'ning ear—
Waited I knew not what, as one will wait
   The coming of a step they know is near.

And when the day waned into purple eve,
   And shadows chill were dropping down to earth,
I knew the happy day was lost to me—
   The day that ushered in the Saviour's birth.
I heard the children shouting at their play,
   Sweet voiced and happy. How it mocked my grief
To hear a laugh from hearts that never ached,
   Knowing mine own could never find relief!

I watched the sun, slow sinking in the west,
   With eyes that seemed not mine, so dull were they,
And pitied the dead heart within my breast,
   So passionless and void of life it lay.

I thought how once I read a foolish tale
• Of sorcerer dread who turned a heart to stone,
And never more, thro' weight of human grief,
    Anguish or pain, it echoed back a moan.
I wondered if some strange magician art
    Could deaden something of the pain I bore,
Or if some happy masquer could not change
    My features to the smile that once they wore.

Again I heard the melody of bells,
    And saw the light along the city street;
I watched the merry groups that met and passed,
    In happy homes with happy hearts to meet.
I drew the curtain of my window close,
    Losing the world, as I had lost the day,
Sick unto death because my heart's one prayer
    Fate answered in its own unfeeling way.

DEAR EYES.

DEAR eyes, if you should chance to fall
    Upon this page I write to-day,
I wonder if within your heart
Would spring a sudden, bitter smart,
    Remembering all you used to say.

I wonder if no keen regret
    For all the wealth of vanished hours,
Would stir your pulse to swifter beat,
Recalling all the days so sweet,
    The happier days that once were ours.

Dear eyes, that learned a cruel look—
    Cold heart, that turned another way,
You never knew the wealth you lost,
Nor what to me the losing cost,
    Your words were only idle play.

Cold eyes, that once could thrill my heart
    With the swift lightning of their blue,
No more I feel the tender lance,
No more I tremble at their glance,
    The tale they told me was not true.

UNDER THE ELM.

SING to me, gentle summer wind,
    Of the beautiful days I lost,
Ere the track of my shining angel
    By sin was ever crossed.
Sing of the far-off summers,
    And woo me back to the hours
When my heart reflected the sunlight,
    And tears were as April showers.

I lie in the elm's broad shadow,
    And see through the branches green
A glimpse of the sky above me,
    A blue and silvery sheen ;
I catch the low, sweet warble
    Of a bird that sings a-near,
A tremulous song of happy love
    With never a note of fear.

The air is all a-tremble
    With songs of a thousand things,
And glancing athwart the sunlight
    I see their shining wings.

And over the fragrant meadow,
  On the fitful breezes borne,
There floats to my ear a thrilling note
  Blown out from a distant horn.

Against my trailing garments
  The beautiful grasses lean,
And down by the elm roots' tangle
  The mosses are cool and green ;
And a rapturous song of thanksgiving
  Wells up from my heart's deep core,
To the Giver of song and sunshine
  And summer's bountiful store.

My soul is sailing away to-day
  On a silvery summer sea ;
The isles of hope that were dim with mist
  Seem fairer and nearer to me.
I wonder if, like the rosy sky,
  Whose color is turning to gray,
My visions will lose their golden light
  As night o'ershadows the day.

SOLDIERS' GRAVES.

WHEN the sweet May comes smiling
Up the southern slopes, and dropping
At her feet the daisy stars, to twinkle
In the grass, as planets in the blue above ;
When lilacs white and purple scent
The air, and tulips flame along the
Borders gay like banners of some fairy
Host ; and when the orchards are
In bridal bloom, and every breath
Of the young year shakes down
A silvery rain of scented leaves
Upon the lap of the dear mother
Earth, who folds away the snowy
Veil, content to know that under
The white fragrance of the laden
Bough was born the promise of the
Perfect fruit :

When all the earth is
Set to cadences of sweetest harmony,
And praise goes up from every heart

In soundless songs of full thanksgiving,
It is but meet, in this most radiant
Time, to gather from earth's green
Bosom the flowers she paints in
• Many-colored dyes, each tint the
Sweet reflection of some vanished
Joy ; and in their full luxuriance
Offer them, a fragrant sacrifice, and
Tender tribute to the honored dead.

Above their dreamless slumber, in
The low tents where summer winds
Stir not the heavy curtains, and at
Whose doors the snowy symbol of a
Truce is set, we walk with reverent
Tread. No more the loud alarm or
Bugle call shall rouse them to
The charge. No trumpet blast,
Or clash of cymbals loud, or
Recreant banner flying to the breeze,
Shall stir again the silent pulses
Of the dead who rest from life's
Great battle. Across the breasts
Where surging tides of passion and
Of wild ambition swept and
Quickened the dull heart-throbs

To a martial meter, lie white and
Nerveless hands, shorn of their cunning
And their power. Young hands, whose
Grasp upon the flashing steel
Was loosened by a mightier one than
Fame. Young brows that went
Unlaureled to the grave, heroes
Uncrowned, ungarlanded, and
Nameless, to find the guerdon in
The great hereafter, that waits for
Those who go to meet their death for
Some great cause.

With reverent step we strew
The white and crimson roses to symbolize
The stripes of the dear flag for which
They fell, and rare blue violets for the
Starry field of the bright banner they
Upbore mid smoke and carnage ;
White lilies in all purity for the fair
Dawn of peace for which they gave
Their brave young lives to martyrdom
And death—while sweetest strains
-Of melody float out upon the golden
Air of spring-time in dirges for the
Dead. Somewhere within the quarry's
Heart rests the white stone that future

Ages shall rear above their widely scattered
Graves ; meanwhile we gem the sod
With tears, and leave our fading
Offering to wither in silent incense
Above the nation's honored dead.

FADED FLOWERS.

YOU ask me why I keep these faded flowers,
  When all the earth is budding into bloom,
And why with folded hands I sit alone,
  Shutting the sunlight from my quiet room?
I am too tired to gather, if I would,
  The sweet wild flowers and the budding rose,
Tired of the sunshine and the glaring light.
  What you deem a weariness, is sweet repose.

I know my flowers are only withered leaves,
  And yet a subtle fragrance lingers there ;
A hallowed something, linked to brighter days—
  A charm no freshly gathered bud can wear.
You say the orchard boughs are sweetly flushing,
  And royal pansies fleck the borders gay,
And summer sends across the sunny hilltops
  Her kisses on the fragrant breath of May.

Ah me ! I know the white and purple lilacs,
  And where the lilies of the valley grow,
Where tender hyacinth and dainty crocus
  First lift their heads above the winter snow ;

I know how fair the hedges are unfolding,
    And how the orchards scatter their sweet rain,
And something in the thought of all their beauty,
    Comes o'er me with a throb akin to pain.

And yet they can not hold the tender meaning
    That once I read in these poor faded flowers;
They whisper not, in all their fragrant breathing,
    Of happy days and swiftly vanished hours.
Go with young hands and gather your fresh roses,
    Hallowing each garland with your heart's best thought,
Anon you'll find amid the withered treasures;
    A mystic meaning, wondrously inwrought.

CAPTAIN JOE.

COMRADES of the march and camp-fire,
And the thrilling battle-call,
Sitting in the waning daylight,
I 've been thinking of you all.
Fancy has been strangely roaming,
In a dim and backward flight,
And again the 57th has been marshaled for the fight.

I can not tell what trifle set my fancy thus at play;
Perhaps 't was hearing mention made of decoration day.
But somehow, in the twilight here,
Strange visions come and go,
And one that lingers longest,
Is the form of Captain Joe.

I need not call him to your minds,
You never have forgot
The stormy fight at Mission Ridge,
Nor yet the sacred spot
Under the heights of Kenesaw,
Where our brave comrade fell,
Pierced through the heart while leading on
The men he loved so well.

Nor how a heavy sadness
  We had never known before,
Fell on our stricken regiment—
  Reached through our army corps.

For often on the toilsome march,
  O'er rough and dusty road,
Some comrade, fainting by the way,
  Has felt the heavy load
Borne from his weary shoulders
  By the arms so strong and brave,
That scorned promotion from the ranks
  He nobly died to save.

Then, comrades of the old brigade,
  As summers come and go,
Remembering all the marches
  Thro' the heat and thro' the snow,
We'll strew fair flowers above their graves,
  Remembering Captain Joe.

TO ONE AFAR.

ALL the long bright summer day,
   Sweetest friend, I 've thought of thee—
I upon the fair green earth,
   Thou upon the broad blue sea.
I have felt the wondrous power,
   Stronger far than cable chain,
That doth bind our spirits still,
   Though between us flows the main.

Though our paths lie far apart,
   As it were from pole to pole,
Naught can break the golden chain
   Binding kindred soul to soul.
There are those with whom we walk
   In our daily joy or care,
Who are yet so far away
   That they do not hear our prayer.

When thy waiting feet shall press
   Other shores, 'neath other skies,
Would that I were with thee then,
   To enjoy the sweet surprise.

When some glorious work of art
  Thrills thee with its magic power,
Think of one whose life-long dream
  Still hath been of such an hour.

And if thou should'st idly stray
  Where the Avon winds along,
With thy soul enwrapped in thought
  Of the glorious King of Song,
Send some sweet remembrance back,
  Though it be a withered flower ;
I shall know that memory turned
  Homeward in that thoughtful hour.
And I promise thee, dear friend,
  Wheresoe'er thy feet may stray,
For their swift and sure return
  I shall ever hope and pray.

MYSTERY.

BECAUSE the sweet June sunshine flecked the field,
  And summer winds in billowing ripples ran
Along the reedy margin of the stream,
  In mournful music, like a dirge for Pan ;
Because a thousand changeful colors swept
  The sky, that mirrored all the sunset glow,
My thoughts went backward to a by-gone day,
  In sweetest memories of long ago.

Oh wondrous mystery of human life,
  So strangely linked by trifles to the past !
A subtle chord that trembles at a touch,
  As if 't were shaken by the stormy blast.
It must be that some secret golden thread,
  Invisible to our material sight,
Unites us to the ones whom we have loved,
  Transmitting messages in flashes bright.

And I have read upon the sky to-day,
  And in the flashing of the rippling stream,
As sweet a message, and as true a sound,
  As ever came to me in happiest dream.

And so it was—a voice once dear to me
 Came back to-day upon the summer air,
And broke the golden silence of my dream,
 By silver words as softly tuned as prayer.

It whispered, "Tho' the summer roses fade,
 And boundless years divide thy life from mine,
My chainless thought will follow, and await   •
 The some time when my love shall be divine."
The flash of thought, invisible to me,
 Is all a mystery I may not know,
But with its voiceless message it has turned
 The tide of memory to the long ago.

WHAT THE DAISY TOLD ME.

I WALKED to-day in the meadow
   With a sad and doubting heart;
I gathered the sweet wild flowers,
   And idly pulled them apart.

For I heard no news from my lover,
   And my tears fell thick and fast,
As I lived again in memory
   The happy days of the past.

And a bitter doubt kept whispering
   These words in my startled ear:
" He is weary of love's sweet bondage;
   He has worn it less than a year."

I gathered a snow-white daisy,
   And I thought of Marguerite,
And I said it shall be an omen,
   While I heard my heart's quick beat,

As out of my trembling fingers
   I let the white leaves fall,
And said, " He loves me dearly,"
   " He loves me not at all."

But the blood rushed up in a crimson tide
From my heart to my burning cheek,
And filled my soul with a tender joy
Too sweet for my tongue to speak.

For the daisy told-me he loved me,
And raising my happy eyes,
I met the face of my lover,
Who came as a glad surprise.

Bloom on, my beautiful daisy,
With messages sad and sweet;
You held a happy omen for me,
And my joy is all complete.

THE VALEDICTORY.

'T WAS a handsome Baccalaureate,
       With his parchment in his hand,
And he briskly stepped on the platform,
    And took his place at the stand ;
And he swept the sea of faces
    With a glance of his fearless eye,
And a look that was full of triumph,
    And courage to do or die.

There were aunts, and uncles, and cousins,
    Relations full half-a-score—
All good, old-fashioned people
    Who considered " larnin' a bore ;"
And friends who were better posted
    On the needs of the rushing times,
Who knew that knowledge is power,
    And ignorance one of the crimes.

Then the valedictory opened :
    " Obscura per obscurius,"
" Ore rotundo," was his style,
    And momently grew more furious.

" Qui non proficit deficit,"
    Was the young man's rallying-cry ;
And he proved that all were turtles
    Who did n't know how to fly.

He threw up a " pons asinorum "
    Of an English sentence or two,
By way of helping his hearers
    To sit and hear him through ;
But he hurled in Greek and Latin,
    And he did it with such force
That in less than fifteen minutes
    His voice grew weak and hoarse.

But on to the end of the chapter,
    This terrible youth went in,
Raking up the dead languages
    In a way that seemed a sin,
Till his voice grew weak and weaker,
    In wild, incoherent mutter ;
" Hoc tempore," they seized him,
    And bore him home on a shutter.

A sad and terrible warning
    To quoters of Greek and Latin,
The young man died, and the hearers scarce
    Could get from the seats they sat in.

The LL. D.'s and D. C. L.'s,
  A. B.'s and the A. S. S.'es,
Got up an elaborate funeral
  To add to his friends' distresses.
They covered his grave with old Greek " roots,"
  And carved on a stone of granite,
" Vir sapit qui paucit loquitur,"
  And the mourners had to " stan' it."

A SAD STORY.

IT 's about an ancient cannibal man,
    Who came from an island near Japan,
A cannibal man who was tough and old
When Barnum bought him and paid in gold ;
And whether the man or Barnum was sold,
    You will learn in this solemn story.

His teeth were sharp as the teeth of a saw,
And he had two rows in the lower jaw
Filed and polished, and ready for use
On any customer full of juice,
Or the first fine baby that lay around loose,
    For babies were all his glory.

A sad mistake for a cannibal band
To come to an almost babyless land,
For babies are strangely out of style ;
You may travel the country many a mile
Without the light of a baby smile,
    Unless with the Dutch and Irish.

But Barnum kept his man in a cage,
Though he felt quite sure, at the fellow's age,
That his cannibalistic feats were done,
Unless he should eat a man for fun ;
And once on the sly he fed him one,
　Which was n't a wise proceeding.

For having tasted a white man's meat,
He was always ready to kill and eat,
And he looked with longing at rosy girls
Who came to the show in shining curls,
With cheeks like peaches and teeth like pearls,
　And he wondered how they tasted.

It happened once, when the flesh was weak,
That he snatched a bite from a rosy cheek.
When Barnum entered the cage to beat him,
The cannibal thought he had come to treat him,
And so straightway began to eat him,
　Without even salt or pepper.

And though he was stringy and awful tough,
For a good square meal he proved enough.
Alas ! alack ! what a terrible omen !
It teaches to women as well as to showmen,
That whether cannibal, Greek, or Roman,
　Be he ever so old, you can 't trust no man.

"UJIJI."

THE shades of night were falling fast,
When through an African village passed
A man whose hair was white as snow,
Repeating in accents solemn and slow—
"Ujiji."

His back was bent with the burden of years,
His cheeks were furrowed by time and tears;
But still he marched with a solemn tread,
And this was the only word he said—
"Ujiji."

Vainly his friends implored him to cease,
Return to his home and rest in peace;
But he said that rest was not his style,
And he wanted to find the source of the Nile—
"Ujiji."

"Oh, stay with me," said a Zemba chief;
"I will give you a wife and plenty of beef."
He wept as he sadly shook his head,
And this dreadful word was all he said—
"Ujiji."

An African princess, smooth and black,
Without any bustle or useless clack,
Besought him to tarry, with tender smile ;
But the siren tongue could not beguile
                              " Ujiji."

He saw in the huts as he passed by,
The cooks preparing to stew and fry,
And a hungry look came over his face ;
But he said as he quickened his lagging pace—
                              " Ujiji."

A Herald reporter, by name of Stanley,
Thought he would do an act that was manly,
And see for himself if this " living stone "
Had become a "dead beat" in the torrid zone—
                              " Ujiji."

He found him resting his weary head
Under an African " watershed ; "
And when he implored the man to go back,
The answer he got was just this slack—
                              " Ujiji."

There, in the evening, dusty and hot,
The old man sits by his boiling pot,
And ever the natives hear him say,
From set of sun till dawn of day—
                              " Ujiji."

THE TYLER DAVIDSON FOUNTAIN.

Y OU wished me to tell you, dear Susie,
What I saw in the city to-day;
How they unveiled the wonderful fountain,
And set the bright waters to play.
If I were to write you a letter
As long as the great fountain square,
I think I could fill up another
And s till have material to spare.

I went to the square at eleven,
The seats were all filled long before;
I stood all unknown and unknowing,
While the crowd surged behind and before.
I was once in the arms of a Teuton,
And once I reposed on a Celt,
And once got a terrible squeezing
From an arm very near to my belt.

I peered over burly, broad shoulders,
And peeped between brown heads and gray;
Oh, the balm of a thousand flowers
Would fail by the smells of that day!

There was one burly tub of old lager
   Came bouncing against me full tilt,
And I thought for one terrible moment
   At least a whole vat had been spilt.

But he righted at once and stood puffing,
   Precisely like one of those tugs
That steam into port at Chicago,
   That town of divorces and plugs.
But the flags that we love were all flying,
   And the silvery notes of the band
Sweetly fell on the air of October,
   That smiled in its beauty so bland.
I tried to get near to the speakers,
   But never a word did I hear—
'T was a kind of " dumb orator " business,
   As good for the far as the near.

I saw on the orator's rostrum
   The Queen City's strength and backbone,
The mayor in all of his glory,
   And the " truly good" man on his throne—
The wealth and the wisdom together,
   The bone and the sinew of life ;
For once they had met on one platform,
   Forgetting all party and strife.

But soon I could see by the gestures
   That the climax was nearly at hand—
The ominous hush of the people,
   The silence that fell on the band.
I had almost forgotten to mention
   An ode, which they said was by Cist.
(I 'm afraid, when it goes to oblivion,
   Its presence will never be missed.)

Just here, at the wave of a 'kerchief,
   The veil of the fountain was rent,
And the sun with a halo of glory
   Its charm to the spectacle lent ;
The water rose higher and higher,
   And soon from the outstretching hand
The Genius poured down like a blessing
   The streams that shall gladden the land.

I was just gushing over with gladness,
   But no one was near that I knew ;
So I kept all my thoughts in a bundle
   On purpose to send them to you.
I shall never attempt to describe it,
   It 's out of the range of my pen ;
When you see it you 'll know all its beauty,
   Do n't try to imagine till then.

There 's a regular queen of a woman,
    That is n't ashamed of her charms,
Who stands on the top of the fountain,
    With beautiful, broad-reaching arms.
There 's another that 's not over-modest,
    Just bringing her boy for a splash ;
I do n't think 't would spoil the artistic
    If he wore a broad flowing sash.

You know, dear, that I 've never traveled,
    And do n't know how such things should be ;
But I do n't think the masses who go there
    Are used to a style quite so free.
There 's a fellow who sits at one corner
    That seems in a terrible way,
With snakes in his boots, I imagine,
    For his countenance thus seems to say :

" Take warning by me, all ye topers ;
    In water had I found delight
The serpent had not coiled around me,
    And brought me to such a sad plight."
But I told you I could not describe it,
    And not a word more will I write ;
But of all the bright scenes I have witnessed,
    The brightest I am sure was that night.

The windows were blazing with candles,
  The streets were alight with red fire,
And the Genius loomed up through the splendor,
  Like a queen on a funeral pyre.
And I, like a princess enchanted,
  Had quite lost the use of my tongue—
You know that is something unusual,
  Considering the way it is hung.

I shall have to postpone till next letter
  What I thought of Janauschek's Medea ;
If my Jason had acted as hers did,
  I am sure that I should n't be here.
But my eyelids are drooping and heavy,
  I really must come to a close ;
Good night, dearest Sue, and God bless you,
  And may you most sweetly repose.

SADDEST WORDS.

ONE of earth's sweetest singers counted once.
And classed life's lamentable sounds—
Classed and appraised its "yea and nay,"
Its jarring discords and its "well-a-day ;"
And out of all the bitterest words to hear,
The words that strike too deep to find a tear
   Were these : " Loved once."

In careless days gone by I read the song—
Read it with idle and unspeculating eyes,
The while I held within my hand a treasure—
One that I prized beyond all earthly measure,
Nor knew that it had slipped beyond my grasp
Until I reached, in vain, once more to clasp
   Only these words : " Was once."

Then with a swift remembrance came to me
The words from those mute lips, silent so long,
" Oh, say not so," least then, when life is shriven
Of those who sit and love you up in heaven,
Whose prayers have met your own,
Whose smiles for you have shown
   " We loved them once."

" Was once " the dearest friend.   Ah me !
Dear friends are for eternity—
Not for the years that change,
But for the shining Heaven beyond the range
Of tears that drop above unanswering clay,
And cold farewells more bitter e'en than they,
    Coldest of all, " Was once.

(GOOD-BYE.)

IT was sweet to hold your hands,
 Looking in your earnest eyes,
Singing you my simple rhymes,
 List'ning to your glad replies.

It was sweet to know your heart
 Answered to my own heart's beat,
As our sweetest dreams of Heaven.
 Oh my dear one, this was sweet!

Sweet to know you heard my voice
 Knocking at your sacred door,
At whose threshold stranger feet
 May not hope to enter o'er.

But my songs are finished now,
 And I turn to quit the place,
With a backward, longing look,
 Praying for your tender grace.

Lingers there one echo sweet—
Trembles one regretful sigh,
With the clasping of my hand,
And my faltering, low good-bye?

FINIS.

www.ingramcontent.com/pod-product-compliance
Lightning Source LLC
Chambersburg PA
CBHW020554270326

41927CB00006B/840

9 7 8 3 7 4 4 6 8 5 2 3 8